God or Lord?

Acts 19:20
Translation Error in the KJB?

With a bonus discussion on
Hope or Faith?
Hebrews 10:23

By Dr. Steve Combs

Published by
The Old Paths Publications
www.theoldpathspublications.com

ISBN 979-8-9928358-1-6

The Author may be contacted by writing:
bpsg.scombs@gmail.com

All Bible quotations are from the Word of God
the Authorized Version (the King James Bible).

Published in the USA by
The Old Paths Publications
www.theoldpathspublications.com

Contents

Dedication

The book is dedicated to my precious wife who has loved me and helped me for over forty years. I thank God for her and for His mercy in giving her to me.

Other Books by Dr. Steve Combs

Election and Predestination: Ephesians 1:4-5
   The real Biblical truth about election and predestination.

Parallel Greek Received Text and King James Version New Testament:
   The TR is one column; the KJB is the second column

The New Testament: The Greek Textus Receptus Global Edition:
   Just the Greek text in large readable type, paper and hardcover

A Practical Theology of Bible Translating:
   What the Bible says about translating it into the world's languages

A Practical Guide to Bible Translation Projects:
   How to set up conduct a successful Bible translation project

The Fellowship of the Mystery: The Book of Ephesians-
   A practical in-depth commentary on the Book of Ephesians

The Power of the Gospel, A Survey of Romans:
   An in-depth survey of the Book of Romans

The Translator's Greek Grammar of the Textus Receptus:
   A Greek grammar of the New Testament based on the Textus Receptus rather than the modern Critical Text

The Legacy Standard Bible and the Questions It Creates:
   An answer to the problems created by the new Legacy Standard Bible-What is God's Hebrew Name, Are Christians Servants or slaves?

So Shall My Word Be:
   Using Biblical Principles to Judge the Modern Bible Versions Movement

God or Lord?

Acts 19:20
A Translation Error in the KJB?

Acts 19:20 is a verse that contains a controversial translation in the KJB. It is a difficult problem. It's surprising that there has not been more said about it. At the mildest, critics have characterized it as a difference between the King James Version and the Greek Received Text. It could be far worse, a translation error. The verse reads:

So mightily grew the word of God and prevailed.

The problem with this verse is the word "God" and the fact that the Greek text does not use the normal word that is translated "God." The normal Greek word for "God" is θεος, *theos*. The word used in Acts 19:20 is κυριος (*Kurios*), which is normally translated "Lord." So, according to the critics the translation *should be* "**word of the Lord**," *rather than* "**word of God**." On the surface, the only logical conclusion seems to be that the KJB is in error here. The KJB is not an accurate translation, at least not in this verse. There are others who do not agree and defend the translation choices in the KJB.

It is clear and unmistakable that the KJB has "God" and the Greek Received Text has Kurios (usually translated *Lord*). That is indisputable. On the surface, it also seems certain that this verse is proof that the King James Version is not inerrant. Some, who say Acts 19:20 is an incorrect translation, will also say that the KJB is an accurate translation. However, the word "accurate" means "inerrant." Therefore, if Acts 19:20 is not correct, the KJB is neither inerrant nor accurate. There have been some who find certain ancient manuscripts and translations which read *theos* or a translation of *theos*, in this verse. However, we accept the Received Text as the preserved Word of God in the Greek language. The Received Text has gone through many editions, but no editor was ever led to change *Kurios* to *theos*. Scrivener edited the Received Text to match the KJB (1881). Not even he would change it. So, we accept the Greek text as being correct.

However, this does not end the argument. There is another side of the coin to examine. The real question is whether the word Kurios *always and only* is to be translated "Lord" when applied to God or the Lord Jesus Christ. Put another way, *can Kurios ever correctly be translated "God?"* I would say that most people who read Greek would say no. All of us who have attended Greek elementary school have been taught that *Lord* is THE one and only way to translate Kurios, when it applies to God the Father or the Lord Jesus Christ. Therefore, they say, the *only right way* to translate Acts 19:20 is "the word of the Lord." If Kurios *can be translated* "God," then the KJB *is accurate* and the translation of Acts 19:20 is not different from the Received Text.

Many of us have done some study in Greek beyond Greek elementary school and we have discovered that Greek words are often far more flexible than we initially learned. Some words carry general meanings that can be translated many ways in different contexts. These words do not always have a set and certain meaning and translation in all contexts. These words must be translated according to the context. Doing so is not always easy. One such word is *ekenosen*. The word means "to *make empty*, that is, (figuratively) to *abase, neutralize, falsify."* The word has a base definition, but it applies differently in a figurative sense according to the context. Modern versions translate this literally (sometimes literal means elementary) in Philippians 2:7, "emptied himself." The KJB translates it "made himself of no reputation." The KJB also variously translates the word "made void" and "made of none effect." These various translations of the same word all carry an element of "make empty, neutralize" but the translation must be refined according to the context.

Another example is the Greek word *yinomai.* This word is one of the most flexible words in the New Testament. The basic meaning of the word is "cause to be" and "to become" (Strong's). Once again this word *must* be translated according to its meaning *in the context.*

In the KJB, it is variously translated: it came to pass, made, done, become, forbid, been, arose, being, be fulfilled, be married (Rom. 7:3-4), brought, cometh, doing, grow, had, have, past, preferred, seemed, showed, trembled, waxed, wrought, assembled, divided, finished, and others. Once again, there is an element of "becoming" in each of these (in the context), but the word cannot be translated literally in the contexts. Take, for instance, Romans 7:3-4 where the word is translated "be married." The verse more literally reads, "So then if, while her husband lives, **she _becomes_ to another man**, she shall be called an adulteress."   The phrase "she becomes to another man" makes no sense in English nor would it be proper to translate it that way. What does she become to the other man? The context is marriage. She "becomes" a wife. So, the KJB translators correctly chose to translate it "be married."

How flexible is Kurios? Can it be properly translated "God?" That is the question we will seek to examine in this article. Kurios also has basic meanings which widen its translation possibilities.

Basic Definitions

First, let's take a look at the basic definitions of Kurios given in lexicons, such as Strong's and Thayer. Let's take a close look at how lexicons handle the word _Kurios_.

1) **Strong's Hebrew and Greek Dictionaries** defines it this way:
   "From κῦρος kuros (_supremacy_); _supreme_ in authority, that is, (as noun) _controller_; by implication _Mr._ (as a respectful title)."
2) **Thayer's Greek Definitions** expands the meaning a bit:
   "he to whom a person or thing belongs, about which he has power of deciding; master, lord" and "this title is given to: God, the Messiah."
3) **The _Abbott-Smith_ Lexicon** says, "having power, authority...lord, master."
4) **Greville Ewing Lexicon 1827:**
   "This term may be given to any person, in whom is vested, (or in courtesy supposed to be vested) property, authority, or right of any kind But when employed in Scripture in an inferior signification, it is accompanied by

some adjunct, qualifying and defining the relation. In other cases it ordinarily denotes the *Supreme Being.* In the LXX it is used to translate אדני *adonai* and יהוה *Jehovah,* and in the N. T. it is applied to the Lord Jesus Christ." (Emphasis-Author)

5) **James Donnegan, Greek English Lexicon, 1833:**
   "Κύριος, ου, ὁ, a proprietor; a possessor; a master; one who has power, or authority over others-in reference to that over slaves δεσπότης is used; κύριος, for a father, a husband, *a Divinity*." (Emphasis-Author)

The word *Kurios* is basically a word that speaks of authority; sometimes supreme authority. It can be applied to both men and God. The KJB translates it with words like sir, master, owner, lord (applied to men), and Lord (applied to God). Since it is translated in various ways and applies to an individual with great, even supreme, power and authority, perhaps it could be translated "God" in the right context. The vast majority of times this word is used in the New Testament, it is translated "Lord" or a variation of it. Once, in Acts 19:20, it is translated "God." The word implies someone who is supreme in authority and of great power. It is applied to both God the Father and to Jesus Christ. Two of the above lexicons specifically define the word as God: "Supreme Being" (i.e. God) and "a Divinity" (i.e. God). I believe that it is valid to translate the Greek word Kurios as "God" for the following reasons.

#1 The KJB Translators Were in Good Company

The reading "word of God" in Acts 19:20 is not unique to the King James Version. It has been pointed out that this same translation was typical of the previous English translations. The first English translation from Hebrew and Greek was done by William Tyndale. From 1524 to 1536 (his death) he translated the New Testament and a large part of the Old Testament. After his death up until the King James translators began to translate in 1604, there were several English translations. Producing these versions took a period of about one hundred years. Tyndale's translation of Acts 19:20 was "word of God." The same translation was in Matthew's Bible (1537), The Great Bible (1540), The Bishops Bible (1568), and the Geneva Bible (1587).

Not only do these translations handle Acts 19:20 the same way the KJB does, but the translators of these versions agreed with the forty-seven King James translators. Couple the fact that these men lived over a period of more than one hundred years with the carefulness and knowledge of the KJB translators. In all their scholarship, they believed it proper to translate *kurios* this way. They translated the word *kurios* as "lord" hundreds of times and they translated it as "God" only one time. They did not translate kurios as "God" carelessly. They did it deliberately, on purpose. We don't know what their purpose and reasons were, but we can reasonably assume they had good ones. These things don't prove that their choice was correct, but it gives a reasonable assurance that it could be. All the other translators independently made the same translation choice. No doubt it was consistent with the scholarship of the day. The Hebrew and Greek learning in the sixteenth and seventeenth centuries came from Jews and Greeks who came from the east, many of them fleeing the Ottoman Turk takeover of the Byzantine Empire. There was present among all these men a level of learning in oriental languages and cultures that today's scholars should envy.

#2 The Testimony of Others

Those who say that there is a translation error in the KJB in Acts 19:20 or who just say there is "difference" are merely voicing their opinions about the matter. Their statement does not make either opinion so. There are other learned individuals who have studied this and other issues regarding the Greek word *kurios*. One of those is Dr. Jeffrey Khoo, Academic Dean of Far East Bible College in Singapore. Regarding Acts 19:20, he said:

> The KJB is not a mistranslation, and does not differ
> from the TR. The Greek word kurios can be translated
> in a number of ways depending on the context. It can
> be rendered "Lord", "master", "Sir", "God", or
> "owner". (see The Complete Word Study Dictionary:
> New Testament, 900-1). Acts 19:20 certainly allows
> for "God" instead of "Lord" since the context is
> speaking of the Word of God as a whole. If it is
> rendered as "the word of the Lord" it might be
> construed as some specific word from Jesus instead

of God's Word or the Holy Scriptures in general. In any case, whether it is "the word of God", or "the word of the Lord", both are perfectly acceptable translations of the original.

Another writer states that the term kurios, when applied to Jesus is meant in the highest possible sense, which is God. In his book, *Christian Theology, 2nd Edition,* Millard J. Erickson, Seminary Professor, states:

> There is a more general argument for the deity of Christ. The New Testament writers ascribe the term κυριος (*kurios*-"Lord") to Jesus, particularly in his risen and ascended state. While the term can most certainly be used without any high Christological connotations, there are several considerations that argue that the term signifies divinity when it is applied to Jesus. First, in the Septuagint κυριος is the usual translation of the name יהוה (Jehovah) and of the reverential ארני (Adonai) which was ordinarily substituted for it. Further, several New Testament references to Jesus as "Lord" are quotations of Old Testament texts employing one of the Hebrew names for God (e.g., Acts 2:20-21 and Rom. 10:13 [cf. Joel 2:31-32]; 1 Peter 3:15 [cf. Is. 8:13]). These references make it clear that the apostles meant to give Jesus the title *Lord* in the highest sense. Finally, κυριος is used in the New Testament to designate both God the Father, the sovereign God (e.g., Matt. 1:20; 9:38; 11:25; Acts 17:24; Rev. 4:11), and Jesus (e.g., Luke 2:11; John 20:28; Acts 10:36; 1 Cor. 2:8; Phil. 2:11; James 2:1; Rev. 19:16). William Childs Robinson comments that when Jesus "is addressed as the exalted Lord, he is so identified with God that there is ambiguity in some passages as to whether the Father or the Son is meant (e.g., Acts 1:24; 2:47; 8:39; 9:31; 11:21; 13:10-12; 16:14; 20:19; 21:14; cf. 18:26; Rom. 14:11)." For Jews particularly, the term κυριος suggests that Christ was equal with the Father.

It is clear that one meaning of kurios, when it is applied to Jesus Christ, is "God." 1 Corinthians 12:3 tells us: *"Wherefore I give you to understand, that no man speaking by the Spirit of God calleth Jesus accursed: and that no man can say that Jesus is the Lord, but by the Holy Ghost."* No one can call Jesus "the Lord" unless it is by the Spirit of God. To call Jesus "the Lord" is to call Jesus "God." The meaning is the same. The term "the Lord" obviously means "God." Therefore, one definition of the Greek term kurios is "God" when it is applied to Jesus or God the Father.

#3 Kurios is Equivalent to Jehovah

Several writers have equated the term kurios with Jehovah of Old Testament Hebrew. Dr. Erickson made that statement in the quote above. Another such source is *The Complete Word Study Dictionary,* by Dr. Spiros Zodhiates in the New Testament, which says, "*kúrios*; gen. *kuríou*, masc. noun from *kúros* (n.f.), might, power. Lord, master, owner. Also the NT Gr. **equivalent for the OT Hebr. Jehovah**." (Emphasis is mine.)   Vine's Expository Dictionary of New Testament Words puts it this way: "kurios is the Sept. and NT representative of Heb. Jehovah ('LORD' in Eng. versions), see Mat 4:7; Jam 5:11, e.g., of adon, Lord, Mat 22:44, and of Adonay, Lord, Mat 1:22; it also occurs for Elohim, God, 1Pe 1:25."

This is more significant than it may seem on the surface. The great objection to the idea that kurios equals Jehovah is that the Old Testament translates Jehovah as "LORD" not "God." This would be devastating to any argument that kurios can be translated "God," if Jehovah can only be translated "Lord." That is, it would be devastating, if it was true. It is not true.

Yes, Jehovah is translated in the Old Testament as "LORD;" but, not always. It is translated that way in hundreds of Old Testament passages. However, it is also translated "God" in several places (e.g., Gen.6:5; Ex. 23:17; Ex. 34:23; 2Sam.12:22). In the formula, "Lord God" the Hebrew is usually "Adon Jehovah" or a variation. Adon is translated "Lord" and Jehovah is translated "God" in Exodus 23:17 and Exodus 34:23. However, in Genesis 6:5 and 2 Samuel 12:22, Jehovah stands alone and is translated "God" in the KJB. *"And **GOD (Jehovah)** saw that the wickedness of man was great in the earth, and that every imagination of the thoughts of his heart was only evil continually"* (Gen. 6:5).

Regarding the name Jehovah, the *The Complete Word Study Dictionary* says this:

> The word refers to the proper name of the God of Israel, particularly the name by which He revealed Himself to Moses (Exo 6:2-3). The divine name has traditionally not been pronounced, primarily out of respect for its sacredness (cf. Exo 20:7; Deu 28:58). Until the Renaissance, it was written without vowels in the Hebrew text of the Old Testament, being rendered as YHWH. However, since that time, the vowels of another word, *ᵃḏōnāy* (H136), have been supplied in hopes of reconstructing the pronunciation. Although the exact derivation of the name is uncertain, most scholars agree that its primary meaning should be understood in the context of God's existence, namely, that He is the "I AM THAT I AM" (Exo 3:14), the One who was, who is, and who always will be (cf. Rev 11:17). Older translations of the Bible and many newer ones employ the practice of rendering the divine name in capital letters, so as to distinguish it from other Hebrew words. It is most often rendered as LORD (Gen 4:1; Deu 6:18; Psa 18:31 [32]; Jer 33:2; Jon 1:9) but also as GOD (Gen 6:5; 2Sa 12:22) or JEHOVAH (Psa 83:18 [19]; Isa 26:4). The frequent appearance of this name in relation to God's redemptive work underscores its tremendous importance (Lev 26:45; Psa 19:14 [15]). Also, it is sometimes compounded with another word to describe the character of the Lord in greater detail (see Gen 22:14; Exo 17:15; Jdg 6:24).

Now we are finally venturing beyond Greek elementary school and boldly stepping into advanced learning. If kurios is the New Testament equivalent to Jehovah (and it absolutely is) and Jehovah in Hebrew is "a noun meaning God" and Jehovah is properly translated "God" in the Old Testament then the Greek word kurios most certainly *can* be rendered "God" in English.

There is further evidence of this. The quotes we have been reading above, have also informed us that Kurios is used in the Old

Testament Greek version (often called the Septuagint) to translate the Hebrew word Jehovah (LORD, God). What is often used and referred to as the so-called Septuagint is the Old Testament of an ancient manuscript known as Vaticanus. It is called this because it is kept in the Vatican Library. Vaticanus is a corrupt manuscript with many errors, additions, etc. However, that does not negate its significant in this discussion. The date of this manuscript is uncertain, but the writing of the manuscript took place at a time when New Testament Greek was known. The writer (s) of Vaticanus was no stranger to Greek and he certainly knew how the Greeks used their words and he knew how the church used Greek words.

The Greek Old Testament of Vaticanus freely uses the word *kurios*. Jehovah in the Hebrew Old Testament is regularly translated as *kurios* in the Greek Old Testament and in the New Testament quotes of the Old Testament. Remember, in one of our examples above, Exodus 23:17, "adon Jehovah" is used and translated "Lord God" in the KJB. In the Greek Old Testament, the words *kurios theos* are used; *kurios for Lord and theos for Jehovah (God)*. Theos is the Greek word for God. In that case, the Hebrew *Jehovah* was translated into Greek as *God*. This was done by the Holy Spirit when He inspired the New Testament. *Kurios* is the equivalent of Jehovah. Therefore, *Kurios* can be translated *God*.

Since Jehovah is translated God and Lord and it is the equivalent of kurios, then kurios also means God and Lord.

#4 Old Testament Quotes in the New Testament

The New Testament quotes or refers to hundreds of verses from the Old Testament. Hidden within those quotes is the final answer to our question. Unfortunately, there is a lot of confusion and ignorance among Christians as to the nature of these quotes. They are generally dismissed by simply saying that they were quotes from the Septuagint, the Old Testament Greek version, not from the Hebrew Old Testament. If they are viewed this way, Christians may miss a great deal of the power and significance of these quotes. I have majored in calling the Septuagint "so-called" and "the Greek Old Testament," because there is a lot of disagreement about whether the Septuagint ever existed or not. The Septuagint was supposed to have been translated before Christ, about 250 BC. There is no direct evidence that this ever took place. There is manuscript evidence of complete Old Testament translations into Greek after Christ was born, but not before.   All of them were written many years after the New Testament was finished; far too late to be used for quotes in the New Testament, but just in time to *copy* quotes *from* the New Testament. So, the Septuagint does not explain the Old Testament quotes in the New Testament. Besides, the quotes in the New Testament do not match the so-called Septuagint. The New Testament quotes the Hebrew Old Testament.

The quotes of the Old Testament in the New Testament come in various types.   There are many direct and indirect quotes. By indirect quote, I mean a quote that is merely a paraphrase of the teaching of one or more Old Testament verses or a teaching which appeals to one or more Old Testament passages for confirmation or proof. There are allusions and possible allusions. An allusion is "a passing or casual reference; an incidental mention of something, either directly or by implication" (dictionary.reference.com).   One example of allusion is Matthew 12:42, *"The queen of the south shall rise up in the judgment with this generation, and shall condemn it: for she came from the uttermost parts of the earth to hear the wisdom of Solomon; and, behold, a greater than Solomon is here."* The Scripture alluded to is 1 Kings 10:1, *"And when the queen of Sheba heard of the fame of Solomon concerning the name of the LORD, she came to prove him with hard questions."* Matthew 12:42 is not intended to be a direct quote. It is intended to be an application of 1 Kings 10 to the present situation in the Lord's life.   There are many allusions in the New Testament.

Another type of quote is similar to an allusion. It is a teaching which appeals to Old Testament Scripture for support. Of course, we do this all the time in teaching and preaching. We make a statement and then refer to what is written for proof. Many times, we don't quote the actual Scripture, but, rather, we paraphrase it.   The Scripture says...then we put it in our own words. The New Testament does something similar. For example, Romans 2:24 says, *"For the name of God is blasphemed among the Gentiles through you, as it is written. "* Here it says, "as it is written," but you will not find this statement, as it is, anywhere in the Old Testament. Instead, you will find Ezekiel 36:20, *"And when they entered unto the heathen, whither they went, they profaned my holy name, when they said to them, These are the people of the LORD."* You will also find Isaiah 52:5, *"Now therefore, what have I here, saith the LORD, that my people is taken away for nought? they that rule over them make them to howl, saith the LORD; and my name continually every day is blasphemed."* This is one of the New Testament equivalents of proof-text teaching.

On the other hand, there are also direct and true quotes from the Hebrew Old Testament. To illustrate, one such quote is in Matthew 1:23, *"Behold, a virgin shall be with child, and shall bring forth a son, and they shall call his name Emmanuel, which being interpreted is, God with us."* This verse is quoted from Isaiah 7:14, *"Therefore the Lord himself shall give you a sign; Behold, a virgin shall conceive, and bear a son, and shall call his name Immanuel. "*

One can readily notice that Matthew 1:23 is not completely the same. There are differences. Matthew 1:23 says "shall be with child" and Isaiah 7:14 says "shall conceive." Matthew 1:23 says "shall bring forth a son" and Isaiah 7:14 says "bear a son." This is typical of many of the Old Testament verses that are quoted in the New Testament. How do we explain this? Well, that's actually quite easy. There are at least two reasons why this happens.

The first reason is that this is not just a quote; it is a Bible translation. Remember, God inspired both Old and New Testaments. He inspired the Old in Hebrew (with a little Aramaic) and the New in Greek. Whenever anyone, even the original author, takes something written in one language and puts it into another language, it is translation. If I write something in English and then write it in German, I have translated my own words. In this case, God has translated his Old Testament Hebrew words into Greek. However, it gets more complicated than that. Men have entered the picture and translated God's words into English. So, you have three languages involved: Hebrew, Greek, and English. The Hebrew Old Testament was translated into Greek. The Hebrew was translated into English and the Greek was translated into English. Now, we are comparing English with English. Any translation between two languages can cause minor word differences or differences in grammar or differences in word order. However, the meaning remains the same if the job has been done right. So, in Matthew 1:23, we have "with child" instead of "conceive," but the meaning is the same. We also have "bring forth a son" instead of "bear a son," but the meaning is the same.

Second, one of the reasons that these quotes are truly helpful to us is that the author of the original and the translation is God. God is the author of the statements in both the New Testament and the Old Testament. When God inspired the New Testament, He knew the exact meaning and intent in the mind of the author of the Old Testament. Therefore, He was able to reveal truth and meaning in the translation that He did not reveal the first time or He was able to confirm the truth of the first statement. Herein lies the true significance of Matthew 1:23. You see in Isaiah 7:14, the Hebrew word for virgin is *'almah*. The word means a virgin or a young woman, unmarried or a newlywed (Brown, Driver-Briggs Hebrew Definitions). In other words, the meaning is uncertain, at least in the minds of many today (although it is hard to see how a newlywed young woman getting pregnant is a sign of any kind). However, when God inspired the New Testament, He used the word *parthenos*. The Greek word can *only* mean virgin (Complete Word Study Dictionary). In other words, the quote and translation of Isaiah 7:14 in Matthew 1:23 confirms the meaning of the Hebrew word *almah* and proves that the correct translation of *almah* in Isaiah 7:14 is *virgin*.

Now, let's take these principles and apply them to our question about whether kurios can be translated "God." The key quote related to this question is found in 1 Peter 1:24-25, "*The grass withereth, and the flower thereof falleth away: But the word of the Lord endureth for ever. And this is the word which by the gospel is preached unto you.*" The quote comes from Isaiah 40:8, "*The grass withereth, the flower fadeth: but the word of our God shall stand for ever.*" The verse in the New Testament says "the word of the Lord" (Kurios). The verse in the Old Testament says, "the word of our God" (Elohim=God). If one compares all of 1 Peter 1:24-25 with Isaiah 40:6-8, he will find that it falls into the category of exact quote with minor differences. Further, it reveals new understanding of the meaning of words, just as Matthew 1:23 does.

The Hebrew word for God in Isaiah 40:8 is *Elohim*. This is THE primary Hebrew word for *God*. When it is applied to God, it is always translated "God." It is **never** translated "Lord." Yet, when God translates this word in 1 Peter 1:25, He inspired the word "kurios." Make no mistake. This was a deliberate act on the part of God. If we believe in verbal plenary inspiration, we must come to this conclusion. *God deliberately, on purpose, with benevolence aforethought chose by an act of His sovereign will to translate Elohim into Kurios.* This clearly means that kurios is not just an equivalent for Jehovah, but *it is also* *the equivalent of Elohim, God.* If Elohim can be translated into kurios, then kurios can absolutely be translated into Elohim. Therefore, "God" can be translated into "Lord" and "Lord" can be translated into "God." So, "Kurios" can be translated into "God."

Conclusion

A deeper understanding of the meaning of "kurios" and its connection with Old Testament Hebrew should sauthorettle the question. "Kurios" means "Lord" and it means "God." When Jesus is addressed as "the Lord Jesus Christ," the truth of His person and nature are included in the name. It is equal to saying, the "God-Man Anointed One." Remember, "no man can say that Jesus is "the Lord, but by the Holy Ghost" (1 Cor. 12:3). To call Jesus "the Lord" does not mean that He is our Master only. The many uses of the phrase "the Lord" in both Testaments clearly reveals its meaning as "God." To call Jesus "the Lord" is to call Him "God."

The word "kurios" not only means God, it can be translated *God.* Kurios is the equivalent of the Old Testament Jehovah. Jehovah is translated both "LORD" and "God" in the Old Testament. Since Kurios is the equivalent of Jehovah, then it too can be translated both Lord and God. That Kurios is equal to Jehovah is seen in Luke 20:42, "And David himself saith in the book of Psalms, The LORD said unto my Lord, Sit thou on my right hand." In Hebrew (Ps. 110:1) this is "Jehovah said to my Adon." In the Greek New Testament, it is "Kurios said to my kurios." Kurios is used for both Jehovah and Adon. This verse clearly shows that Kurios is the equivalent of Jehovah, as well as Adon. 1 Peter 1:25 is the same type of example as Luke 20:42. It reveals that kurios is also the equivalent of Elohim (God). The Old Testament (Is. 40:8) says, "The word of Elohim." 1 Peter 1 says, "The word of kurios." The connection here is the same as Luke 20:42. It creates an equivalency. Kurios equals Jehovah. Kurios equals Elohim. Kurios equals "Lord" and "God."

Hope or Faith?
Hebrews 10:23

We received this challenge regarding Hebrews 10:23, "Hebrews 10:23 Let us hold fast the profession of our **faith** without wavering; (for he is faithful that promised;)" –

"The KJV says 'the profession of our faith,' but the TR says 'Elpis,' which is translated as hope in every other place in the KJV (over 50 places). Here is another example where the KJV and the TR simply do not match. It poses no theological or hermeneutic problems, but they are not the same. Without consulting the Greek, a translator would never pick this up from the context."

There is only one possible conclusion to the statement: "Here is another example where the KJV and the TR simply do not match." The King James Bible has an incorrect translation here. It has an error in the translation of *elpis* as *faith* rather than *hope*. Is this true?

Hope is faith. The two words are synonymous. Faith focuses on the object of faith. Hope focuses on the expectation of faith, the reward expected (Heb. 11:6). Hope for a Christian is confident trust in the reward. Faith is an important and inseparable element of a Christian's hope. Let's look at several sources of information to find the real meaning of *elpis*.

<u>1. Lexicons, include the following definitions of *elpis*</u>:

A. Mounce: expectation; hope, Act_24:15; Rom_5:4; meton. the object of hope, thing hoped for, Rom_8:24; Gal_5:5; the author or source of hope, Col_1:27; 1Ti_1:1; **trust, confidence,** 1Pe_1:21; ἐπ' ἐλπίδι, in security, with a guarantee, Act_2:26; Rom_8:20.

B. Complete Word Study, Zodhiates: Of a hope in or on someone, i.e., **trust, confidence**

C. Samuel Loveland, 1828 Lexicon: hope, the object or author of hope; **confidence,** security.

D. John Parkhurst, 1829 Lexicon: Trust, confidence joined with hope; **confidence**, security.

E. John Pickering, 1832 Lexicon: Hope, expectation; beyond expectation; **trust**, fear (his study includes the Greek classics)

F. James Donegan, 1833 Lexicon: Hope, dread, expectation, **reliance**.

G. J. A. Giles, 1840 Lexicon: hope, **confidence**, **reliance**

H. Greville Ewing, 1827 Lexicon: Hope, **trust, confidence,** security, expectation

Elpis is like many Greek words with one or more primary definitions and many minor definitions.

How much of a Greek scholar does one have to become to translate? Pickering studied the Greek classics to come up with definitions. The KJV translators already did the Greek scholarly studies. Greek knowledge in 1611 had come from the Greeks. In fact, it had not been that long since knowledge of Greek was brought to Europe by the Greeks themselves (fleeing from Moslem invasion in the east). These immigrants taught Greek to the Western Europeans. I would rather trust the knowledge of Greek the KJV translators had than any of the modern teachers or books I have had.

<u>2. The Bible:</u>
Hebrews 11:1 *"Now **faith** is the substance of things **hoped** for, the evidence of things **not seen.**"* Hope and faith are tied together. Faith is hope and hope is faith.
Romans 8:24 *"For we are saved by hope …"*

Really? I thought we are saved by faith (Eph. 2:8-9). Galatians 3:26, "For ye are all the children of God by faith in Christ Jesus." Romans 5:1, "Therefore being justified by faith …" We are saved by hope, but hope *is* faith.

<u>3. English Dictionaries, Definition of *Hope*:</u>

A. Merriam-Webster: v.t. to expect with **confidence: trust**

B. Webster 1828: v.t. To place confidence in; to **trust** in with **confident expectation** of good.
noun. Confidence in a future event.

If the translators rendered *elpis* as faith in a single instance out of over 50 uses, then they knew full well the meaning of *elpis* and they must have had good reason to translate it differently in this verse. Here is my perspective on this.

Many Greek words are flexible in their usage, as you know. The principle of **polysemy** teaches that words have **multiple meanings**. The verb form of the noun, *elpis*, is *elpizo*. It was translated "trust," "trusteth," or "trusted" 18 times out of 32. Mounce defines *elpizo* as 1) to hope, expect and 2) to repose hope and confidence in, trust, confide.   *Trust is faith.*   In its definition, the Word Study Dictionary uses these words to define *elpizo*: to hope, expect with desire, to trust in, and confide in.

Elpis, then, is defined as 1) Hope, desire some good with expectation of obtaining it; 2) trust and confidence;   3) hope with expectation;   4) anticipation with pleasure, expectation or confidence. According to Webster, the English word, hope, means to trust in with confident expectation of good. All of this includes an overwhelming element of faith, because trust, expectation, and confidence are faith.

In addition, Romans 8:24 is a cross reference to Ephesians 2:8. Rom. 8:24 says, "For we are saved by hope" and Eph. 2:8 says, "For we are saved through faith." Hope and faith are synonymous, depending on the context. Rom. 8:24 further states, "but hope that is seen is not hope: for what a man seeth, why doth he yet hope for?" To confidently hope and trust for what you cannot see is the definition of faith. "Now faith is the substance of things *hoped for*, the evidence of things *not seen*" (Heb. 11:1). There is an unbreakable connection between the nature of faith and the nature of hope. Faith is hope and hope is faith. Faith is the assurance of hope.

Then there is the context of Heb. 10:23. Verse 22 says, "Let us draw near with a true heart in full assurance of faith." The word faith is pistis in verse 22 and is connected with the elpis of verse 23, which is followed up later in verse 23 with, "for he is faithful (pistos) that promised." The subject under discussion is faith, not merely hope. "Let us draw near with a true heart of faith ... Let us hold fast the profession of our faith ...; (for he is faithful that promised)."

About the Author

Dr. Steve Combs is an ordained minister. He spent his early years in Kentucky, Virginia, and finally Ohio. He was not raised in a Christian home. He had some Christian influence from his grandmother, but that had little effect on him. Due to discussions with a Baptist preacher and a Sunday School teacher, who visited his home, he began to read the Bible. The Word of God had its effect. He came under strong conviction for his sins. A friend invited him to a nearby church during revival meetings. As a result, he received Christ as his Savior.

Since then, there have been major transformations to his life. God called him to preach and enabled a backward shy individual suffering from an inferiority complex to stand before crowds and confidently proclaim the Word of God. God gave him a business background as a CPA. God put him in several ministry positions. He has served as a Bible Institute teacher and Dean, a youth pastor, assistant pastor, and a senior pastor. He holds a BA from Cedarville University and a Doctor of Theology from Covington Theological Seminary.

Currently Steve Combs is Assistant Director and a Global Translation Advisor for Global Bible Translators/ Bearing Precious Seed Global, www.bpsglobal.com, a ministry of Plantation Baptist Church in Plantation, Florida. Global Bible Translators starts and assists Bible translation projects around the world.

He is married and has four married children.

www.ingramcontent.com/pod-product-compliance
Lightning Source LLC
Chambersburg PA
CBHW051340150726
47997CB00004B/1546